Forty Acres
and
Some Dividends

Recovering from a Broken Promise
"Investing for African Americans"

By: Tayvon Jackson

Copyright © 2014 by Tayvon Jackson

40 Acres and Some Dividends
Recovering from a Broken Promise "Investing for African Americans"
by Tayvon Jackson

Printed in the United States of America

ISBN 9781498409292

All rights reserved solely by the author. The author guarantees all contents are original and do not infringe upon the legal rights of any other person or work. No part of this book may be reproduced in any form without the permission of the author. The views expressed in this book are not necessarily those of the publisher.

www.xulonpress.com

TABLE OF CONTENTS

Introduction vii

Chapter 1:   Why Is It So Hard To Think About Retirement? 11

Chapter 2:   Why Invest? 15

Chapter 3:   Treat Investing Like A Bill.......... 19

Chapter 4:   Be Selfish With The Kids' Education 21

Chapter 5:   Prioritize.......................... 25

Chapter 6:   Traditional Ira Vs. Roth 31

Chapter 7:   Do I Need Life Insurance?.......... 35

Chapter 8:   When People Are Scared To Invest, Invest! 39

Chapter 9:   Social Security And Pensions....... 43

Chapter 10: What Is Diversification?............45

Chapter 11: What To Look For In A
            Financial Advisor?.................47

Chapter 12: Be A Boss.........................51

Conclusion 53

INTRODUCTION

"The term, 'forty acres and a mule' is used to explain the compensation that was to be awarded to freed black slaves after the Civil War. Forty acres of land to farm and a mule with which to drag a plow so the land could be cultivated was supposed to be awarded to every black slave as a form of reparations for their tenure or parent's tenure in slavery. This was also so they could sustain themselves after they gained freedom." (blackhistory.com) This promise was never fulfilled.

So you may wonder why I'm writing this book. Many of us feel we are entitled to something, and that certain opportunities in life should be given to us. We fail to take the initiative in our lives and rely on pipe dreams such as lottery tickets or our children becoming professional athletes to support us later in life. We also do a poor job of managing our money.

I'm sure people are reading this and saying they are different and they are smart with there finances, planning for their future, etc. I'm sorry, but maybe this book is not for you. This book is for many African Americans that I've encountered in my career as a financial advisor. From experience, I've heard every excuse in the world from, "I am never going to retire," to, "I'm living paycheck by paycheck, why should I invest my money? I may never live to see it" to, "My friends lost thousands of dollars in the market, are you crazy telling me to invest?" Once again, if this does not apply to you, then I am sorry that you invested in this book, but please share it with a friend who may need it.

Introduction

I'm no millionaire. I can't say that everything I tell you to do is going to make you rich. I do guarantee that if you follow what I say, you will be in a better situation then you are now. If there is one thing that you can take from this book, and apply it to your everyday life, then it's worth it.

From a young age, I always had a curiosity in making money. Why were so many people in my community living paycheck-by-paycheck, working forever, and unhappy? When would the cycle end? *Rule #1: Don't be a victim of circumstance.* No mater what your situation is, there's a way to better yourself.

I grew up in a small town in Waldorf, Maryland. I went to a small school called Mount Saint Mary's University, where I was fortunate enough to play college basketball and triple majored in Math, Business, and Information Systems. Now I work for a great financial company. The reason I got into the financial industry is the exact reason why I'm writing this book: to educate my community on how to make better decisions with their money. I'm sorry this is not a one hundred plus page book, but I designed it so that you could read this within one day, and apply it to your life immediately. This book may rub some people the wrong way and that is okay. Books are not written to please everyone, but designed to put your thoughts and feelings on paper, and to share with the world. It's never too late to learn about investing.

Chapter 1
WHY IS IT SO HARD TO THINK ABOUT RETIREMENT?

As African Americans, we came from a strong culture that believed in hard work; there was never a thought of retirement. Coming from an era of slavery, we worked, worked, worked, and then eventually died. There were no forty acres and a mule given to us. There was also no retirement picture at all, and that mindset has translated into today's culture. We are so concerned about the now—buying the new house, the new car, the latest fashion—that we fail to realize there is a good chance that we won't be able to work forever.

Rule #2: There's a chance something unplanned will cause you to retire sooner than you want. I met a barber who told me that he did not need a retirement plan. He was making great money, with most of it not being claimed on taxes. He planned on being a barber for the rest of his life. Unfortunately, a year later he had a stroke. Sorry this story has no happy ending, but the point is, our health can cause us to retire earlier then we want. With no savings or retirement, we are depending on others and government programs to assist us.

Let me ask you a question: if you quit your job right now, how long would you be able to support your lifestyle? I can admit that retirement is scary. I was only twenty-six at the time of writing this book and I am already thinking about it. What would I do? Where would I live? Could I afford to not work? There's so much uncertainty with Social Security and Pensions, which I will discuss later, that there is a slim chance that no one is going to support you through your retirement. Your retirement is based on your own efforts, and even though you may feel invincible now, one day there will be a time where you can't work any longer. How many years will your money last?

CHAPTER 2
WHY INVEST?

Why do we invest? Is it just to make money? I'm not old but even I could remember a time when I could put twenty dollars in my gas tank and fill it up. Now it costs me nearly sixty dollars. Everything is getting more expensive every single day. Gas, education costs, groceries — why is everything getting so expensive? Do you know one thing that is not going to increase with cost of living? That money you have sitting in the bank. I know a lot of people reading this are old school and still have the occasional box of money on top of the fridge, or would rather bury their cash out back under the tree than invest it in the stock market. What if I told you that being too conservative is just as risky as being too aggressive? What do I mean? The biggest risk of being too conservative is losing your purchasing power. A dollar today is not a dollar tomorrow. If you need one hundred thousand dollars a year to survive in today's dollars, it'll be close to three hundred thousand dollars twenty years from now. Are you prepared for that? What if I told you that if you weren't making at least three percent on your money in the banks, then you are actually guaranteed to lose it? Would you think about your conservative attitude a bit differently?

So where did this conservative mindset come from? In 1982, the life expectancy for an African American man was sixty-five and for women, seventy-three. So investing in cash, CDs, and bonds made sense. Once we retired, we only had to preserve our money for a few years until we were dead.

Fortunately, with better health care, people are living longer, but we still are utilizing these investment vehicles of the past. Many people become more conservative with their investments as they get closer to retirement. As a result, many retirees are running out of money shortly after retirement. You have to expect to live twenty, thirty, even forty years in retirement. In the stock market, you may lose at times, but by not investing, you will never win. *Rule #3: By not investing, you are guaranteed to lose your money.*

CHAPTER 3
TREAT INVESTING LIKE A BILL

What if I told you that if you invest a little bit of money for a long period of time, you would be a millionaire? Would you believe me? Probably not. That's the problem. People have the mindset that you need a lot of money to invest. That is farthest from the truth. When I work with a lot of my clients, I tell them that they have to treat investing as if they are paying their water or cable bill. So I'm sure you didn't think that getting this book would make you spend more money, but it is. You will thank me for this soon. What I want you to do is to make a new bill. This bill is called, "yourself." Pay yourself first.

Rule #4: You are not buying anything; you are just getting a better return on your money. When people talk about investing, they think they are buying something. You know for sure that if your bank told you they were offering eight percent, everyone would go to that bank. The money that you invest is still your money. You are just hoping to get a better return then the bank, and to be able to use it at a later date for a future goal such as retirement, college, etc.

Every month, I want you to pay the "yourself" bill. Start off with a specific dollar amount monthly, and increase accordingly. One thing that you have to make sure that you never do is stop; you can always increase or decrease your monthly amount, but never stop. Just think how mad your kids would be if you stopped paying the cable bill, and they couldn't watch "SpongeBob" or ESPN. Don't ever stop investing in yourself.

CHAPTER 4
BE SELFISH WITH THE KIDS' EDUCATION

Mom: "I'm going to invest in my kid's college because I want him to be a productive citizen in society and not make the same mistakes I made."

Financial Advisor: "That sounds great, but what are you doing for your retirement?"

Mom: "Nothing yet, but once my kid finishes school, I'll focus on me."

If this sounds like you, then I'm sorry. Paying for your child's education is one of the biggest reasons that will cause you to work until you die. If you don't believe me, then read this:

The average private school tuition is around thirty thousand dollars. The cost of education is increasing more than inflation. Translation: college is not getting any cheaper. Education is supposed to be the great equalizer, the one thing that no one can take away, and the one component that can make one person stand out from the others. Don't take this chapter the wrong way. Education is important and I was fortunate to graduate with three majors on an athletic scholarship, but sometimes you have to be a little selfish. Let's say your son wants to go to college. There are multiple ways he can go: he can get an athletic scholarship, an academic scholarship, student loans, grants, apply for financial aid — the opportunities are endless. *Rule #5: There are back-up plans for college, but not for retirement.* Let's say that Momma wants to retire next year. I'm sorry to tell you, but they don't give you loans or scholarships for retirement. That is why you have to be selfish, and your financial future should be your first concern.

> *Note: We all know that our kids come first and most of us would do anything to ensure that they get their proper education. Please keep in mind that planning for a child's education should start at birth to avoid having to make the difficult decision between your retirement and their education.*

Chapter 5
PRIORITIZE

So far, I've told you that you have to pay another bill (the "yourself" bill) and to not help with your kids' college. You may wonder exactly what to focus on when it comes to managing your money and your financial future. What exactly should you be doing then?

1. Contribute to your company's 401K plan.

Find out how much they are matching. If they are matching five percent, put in five percent. If they are putting in ten percent, put in ten percent. Your retirement plan match is the only time that you can get a one hundred percent return on your money because for every dollar you put in, your employer will match you up to that percentage. No stock can consistently beat that.

2. Build an emergency fund.

Life happens; whether it's a storm that damages the home, job loss, car breaking down, or an unexpected illness. The last thing you want to do is tap into your retirement savings. Tapping into your retirement savings could cost you a ten percent early withdrawal penalty and income tax. After you contribute to your match, anything extra should be put into an emergency savings or money market. The rule of thumb is three to six months worth of living expenses. The way you come up with the emergency fund amount is to find out how much money you have coming into the household each month after taxes and multiply it by the appropriate number of months.

3. Contribute more to an IRA or another investment account.

Now that you are contributing up to the match in your 401K, you have your emergency fund, now what? Anything extra that you have should be invested into an individual retirement account (IRA or ROTH explained in the next chapter). You could put the extra money into your 401K, but usually most employer-sponsored plans are limited to the funds that you can invest in. Therefore, I'd rather you be more diversified and invest outside your plan. Investing in IRAs allow you to invest in any company in the world. If you drink Pepsi or eat McDonald's, or shop at Target, you can invest in these company stocks and better position yourself for your financial future. The max for IRA's is $5500 annually as of 2014, and $6500 annually if you are over fifty.

4. College savings plan

Now that we have addressed saving for yourself, we can talk about the kids. Two great vehicles to use are 529 plans and custodial accounts. 529 plans are a tax-free way of saving for education. As long as the child goes to an accredited college or university, all of the earnings in the plan are tax-free. The great thing about it is that anyone can help contribute. This includes friends, family, random strangers — anyone can help. One thing to think about is instead of everyone getting gifts for your child on birthdays and holidays, tell your family and friends to write a check for education.

Custodial accounts are taxable and they are irrevocable gifts that can't be taken back. Many people open custodial accounts for children so that they are not limited to just college. After a custodial account is open, the person who opened the account owns the account. Once the child turns of age, whether eighteen or twenty-one, (plans vary) the money now belongs to them and can't be taken away. This plan doesn't limit you to college.

CHAPTER 6
TRADITIONAL IRA VS. ROTH

Everyone has heard the debate between whether they should have an IRA or a Roth. First of all, you have to be working with earned income to contribute to either. An IRA is a tax-deferred way to plan for your retirement. What does tax-deferred mean? It means that the money goes in *before* tax and you don't pay taxes until you withdraw the money at retirement. The advantage is that while you are working, you are probably making the most money that you can possibly make. Hopefully when you retire, you are not working as hard and may be making less. You would much rather pay the taxes at retirement when you are in a low tax bracket, then while you are working. Another advantage is that if you are under certain income limits, every dollar you put in reduces the amount of money that the government can tax you on. Unfortunately, you have to keep the money in an IRA until you are fifty-nine or it could result in a ten percent penalty. This type of forced savings can also be great because it is not easy access. There are exceptions to the penalties of tapping into your retirement plans such as paying for a first time home purchase, higher education, or unforeseen medical expenses but I won't elaborate on that much. By law, you have to take the money out of your traditional IRA by seventy or you could suffer penalties up to fifty percent.

On the contrary, a Roth IRA is a tax-free way to save for retirement. All the money that is contributed is going in with after tax dollars, which makes it tax-free when it's withdrawn. There are income limitations to contributing to a Roth IRA, so not everyone can contribute (married filing jointly over $191,000 means no contribution can be made). There is no timetable to take the money out of the account because it's already been taxed.

To summarize, the maximum contributions to a traditional IRA and Roth IRA are $5500 a year as of 2014, and $6500 if you are over fifty. If you believe taxes will be lower for you in the future, then maybe an IRA is suitable. If you think taxes may rise or you may make a lot more in retirement than you make now, the Roth would be the best option.

CHAPTER 7
DO I NEED LIFE INSURANCE?

Insurance is a sensitive topic for a lot of people. No one likes having the conversation that they will eventually die. A lot of people don't like paying for something that they will never see paid out. You absolutely need it. Take this as an example. There's a husband and a wife with four children all under the age of eighteen. The husband is the CEO of a company and he makes over $300,000 a year. The wife is a schoolteacher, getting paid roughly $40,000 a year. They have a beautiful home, a dog, and two parakeets — the perfect family with no worries at all. The husband makes good money and feels that retirement is not a top priority. They have a huge house, nice cars, and never have to worry about money, but unfortunately due to their lifestyle, they are spending as much as they make. This family is considered "house poor", meaning they make good income, but have a low net worth due to lack of saving and investing.

One night, the husband doesn't come home because he was killed in an automobile accident with no insurance in place. Right away, the household goes from two incomes to one. Second, the mom is now responsible for getting all of her kids through college, so they now have to rely on student loans and financial aid, possibly a few scholarships. Next, the single income can no longer pay the high mortgage and they will end up losing their house. Finally, she is also responsible for final expenses and burial of her husband. This may be extreme, but this is the typical scenario of what can happen with no life insurance.

Now let's say the husband made the smart decision to get a twenty year/one million dollar policy that costs him as little as $200 a month. Life insurance proceeds are all tax-free, so if you have a million dollar policy, that is how much you will receive.

Back to the example: the wife could send all of the kids to college without having to take out any loans. She can pay off the home if that is what she wants to do. She has enough cash to replace his income for a few years so that the family can get back on their feet. *Rule #6: Deaths in the family are already emotional; don't make them financially emotional as well.*

I'm not really big on permanent insurance unless you get it at a young age and it is cheap, though term life insurance is important. Term insurance is exactly what it states: you pay premiums for a certain term—whether it be ten, twenty, thirty years—and if anything happens to you within this time period, your beneficiaries will get the policy. If nothing happens to you then you don't get anything. It's cheap because most people never end up dying in that term but the reason you buy term is for that peace of mind that if anything were to happen to you, everyone who you wish to protect will be okay financially. Many people end up outliving their term. As a retiree, the house should be almost paid off, and a small permanent policy should be good enough. There is no need to pay extreme premiums when you're eighty and your kids are sixty. *Rule #7: It is much better to have good insurance and not need it, then need it and not have it.*

CHAPTER 8
WHEN PEOPLE ARE SCARED TO INVEST, INVEST!

Unfortunately we come from a society of followers. New trends cause new followers, whether it's social media platforms such as Twitter, Instagram, Facebook, or a new style of clothes. One thing I can say is that if you follow the herd when it comes to investing, you will most likely end up broke.

When people have jobs, the economy is booming, people are smiling and laughing and everything is perfect — that is the worst possible time to invest. Why? When things are going well, most likely the stock market is up. I don't know how much shopping you do, but in any other industry, you shouldn't ever buy when prices are up, and that includes the grocery store, real estate, the mall, or anywhere. The stock market is the only industry that when things are on sale, people leave the store. The right time to make a quality investment is when you have the money available. The key is to invest when the market is low not when it is high.

More times then not, if there is encouraging news about stocks and investments, you probably have missed the boat. In contrast, when the economy is a disaster, there is fear about the world coming to an end, worries about the fiscal cliff, the government shut down — that is the ideal opportunity to invest. Prices are down, no one is buying, and the great thing about it is that when the market does recover, you got a good deal. Think of it as buying winter clothes in the summer. You buy it because it's cheap, no one wants it, and when the winter comes around you are glad you got it at the price you did.

Rule #8: When people are buying, you had better be selling.

CHAPTER 9
SOCIAL SECURITY AND PENSIONS

"I'm going to depend on social security for my retirement."

"I don't need to invest, I'm going to get a check from my company for the rest of my life."

Many times I've seen people not worry about investing at all due to the fact that they think they will be covered by social security and their company pension plan. While this may be true, there's a lot of uncertainty on this topic when it comes to the future. As previously discussed in chapter two, the government does not mind paying you social security for a few years after retirement because they figure you will die soon. Fortunately for us (not for them), the life expectancy has increased tremendously. So the problem arises that social security was not designed for people to be living longer. This is why there is so much uncertainty. With the baby boomers retiring at a rapid pace of eight thousand people a day, social security is being stretched. This is the same problem company pension plans are experiencing, which resulted in many companies starting defined contribution plans, which are retirement vehicles where you have to fund your own retirement in your company's 401K, 403B, 457, TSP, etc. *Rule #9: Only trust your own dollars.*

CHAPTER 10
WHAT IS DIVERSIFICATION?

Rule #10: Never keep all your eggs in one basket.

This rule is overly misinterpreted. Diversification does not mean having your money spread out between three banks and four financial companies. Diversification means investing in multiple products that react different to market scenarios. I would not recommend putting your whole retirement plan in your favorite stock, or the annuity that some salesman pitched you. A bad investor is someone who always looks for the highest return. Unfortunately, the highest returns usually lead to the worst disasters (example: 2008 crash). All you are trying to do with investments are to have okay days. Yes, your friend may say that he did forty percent on XYZ mutual fund, but all that means is that it's going to crash just as hard. Just have okay days by being diversified. You won't always do the best, but you will never do the worst, and that is all you need.

CHAPTER 11
WHAT TO LOOK FOR IN A FINANCIAL ADVISOR?

I may be a little biased in this chapter because I hope everyone reading would give me a chance to help them reach their financial goals. Why would you even need a financial advisor? We don't even like to talk to our friends and family about investing, let alone some stranger with a nice suit. The hardest part of my job is having people get over the fear that not everyone is trying to take advantage of them. All you hear about in the news are stories of people getting scammed. As a race, our culture is hesitant to trust, especially regarding our money.

Why should you think about working with an advisor? First, your time is your most precious asset. The last thing you need to do is look at the market every day when you are supposed to be working, enjoying retirement, or spending time with the family. A good financial advisor gives you proactive calls during good times and bad. A financial advisor should be an extended part of your family, someone who you know, like, and eventually trust. Your advisor shouldn't be a 1-800 number or a call center, but should be able to be distinguished in a crowd. You want an advisor who not only calls you on a stock idea, but sends you "get well soon" cards when you're down, wishes you and your spouse a happy anniversary, happy birthday, asks you how your son's basketball game was, and maybe even show up and support. The financial advisor relationship is not just for your lifetime, it's multigenerational. You want someone who can not only be there for you, but also for your kids, and maybe even your grandkids if you are lucky. You wouldn't do your own surgeries; you hire a surgeon, so don't make the same mistake with your money. Get a financial advisor.

CHAPTER 12
BE A BOSS

I know this topic doesn't exactly relate to what I've been talking about in previous chapters, but I absolutely believe it is worth sharing. What is the difference between people like Bill Gates, Walt Disney, Steve Jobs, and Mark Zuckeburg? They are not working for anyone but themselves.

In order to be that top one percent, you can't work for anyone else, you have to start your own company, be your own boss, and make things happen yourself. I told myself that I would never work a typical job; I would never commute, and would never work harder then someone else and get paid less. There are a lot of platforms out in the market today that can teach you how to have this freedom. Network marketing is a huge business model that has unlimited money making potential and the freedom to do it at your own pace. So I would recommend around your nine to five job, join a network marketing business part time, and when your residual income ends up more then your salary at your real job, then it s time to make changes. *Rule #10: Don't let anyone limit you, be your own boss.*

CONCLUSION

Now that you are finished reading, your financial future is in your hands. It's easy to close this book and never look at it again. One recommendation is to find two to three key points and implement them in your life right away. If you do not have life insurance, think about your family and decide to take out a policy. Do you want to get started with investing? Start by taking fifty dollars a month to pay the "yourself" bill. Financial freedom for tomorrow starts with what you do today.

What are your three takeaways from this book that you will apply tomorrow?

_____

_____

_____

"How many millionaires do you know who have become wealthy by investing in savings accounts? I rest my case." -Robert G. Allen

Special Thanks to Jeff Wilson II for helping with the book title.

Made in the USA
Middletown, DE
08 November 2017